# Trailblazers in the AIR

by Charis Mather

Minneapolis, Minnesota

**Credits**

Images are courtesy of Shutterstock.com. With thanks to GettyImages, ThinkstockPhoto, and iStockphoto. Throughout – GoodStudio, mhatzapa. Cover – SHCHERBAKOV, SERHII, Pretty Vectors, robuart, Na_Studio, Valine Tina, Kobsoft. 4–5, intararit; 6–7, mckenna71, unknown (WikiCommons), HappyPictures; 8–9, Dacian Galea, National Photo Company Collection (WikiCommons); 10–11, Evellean, unknown (WikiCommons); 12–13, alex74, Pretty Vectors, Ziablik, George Rinhart/Corbis via Getty Images; 14–15, John M. Noble (WikiCommons), Olga_Bell, Tartila, ZHUKO, SpicyTruffel; 16–17, Kuch Vasta, Underwood & Underwood (WikiCommons); 18–19, Ziablik, Andy Dingley (WikiCommons); 20–21, John Mathew Smith (WikiCommons), CloudyStock, mckenna71; 22–23, abbydesign, Astarina, Pand P Studio.

**Bearport Publishing Company Product Development Team**

President: Jen Jenson; Director of Product Development: Spencer Brinker; Managing Editor: Allison Juda; Associate Editor: Naomi Reich; Senior Designer: Colin O'Dea; Associate Designer: Elena Klinkner; Associate Designer: Kayla Eggert; Product Development Specialist: Anita Stasson

*Library of Congress Cataloging-in-Publication Data*

Names: Mather, Charis, 1999- author.
Title: Trailblazers in the air / by Charis Mather.
Description: Minneapolis, Minnesota : Bearport Publishing Company, [2024] |
   Series: Our greatest adventures | Includes index.
Identifiers: LCCN 2023002680 (print) | LCCN 2023002681 (ebook) | ISBN
   9798885099578 (hardcover) | ISBN 9798888221327 (paperback) | ISBN
   9798888222775 (ebook)
Subjects: LCSH: Air pilots--Biography--Juvenile literature.
Classification: LCC TL539 .M3234 2024  (print) | LCC TL539  (ebook) | DDC
   629.13092--dc23/eng/20230123
LC record available at https://lccn.loc.gov/2023002680
LC ebook record available at https://lccn.loc.gov/2023002681

© 2024 BookLife Publishing
This edition is published by arrangement with BookLife Publishing.

North American adaptations © 2024 Bearport Publishing Company. All rights reserved. No part of this publication may be reproduced in whole or in part, stored in any retrieval system, or transmitted in any form or by any means, electronic, mechanical, photocopying, recording, or otherwise, without written permission from the publisher.

For more information, write to Bearport Publishing, 5357 Penn Avenue South, Minneapolis, MN 55419.

# CONTENTS

Our Greatest Adventures by Air ...... 4

Jean-Pierre Blanchard.............. 6

Hugo Eckener .................... 8

Orville Wright and Wilbur Wright.... 10

Bessie Coleman.................. 12

Charles Lindbergh ............... 14

Amelia Earhart ................. 16

Amy Johnson .................. 18

Bertrand Piccard and Brian Jones .... 20

Your Air Adventure ............. 22

Glossary ..................... 24

Index ....................... 24

# OUR GREATEST ADVENTURES BY AIR

Have you been in an airplane? At one time, flying in the sky seemed impossible. Now, people travel by air every day.

The first air adventurers took to the skies so we could, too. Let's meet some of these brave people!

# JEAN-PIERRE BLANCHARD

**Born: 1753   Died: 1809**

The hot-air balloon was invented in 1783. Soon after, a French man named Jean-Pierre Blanchard started **touring** with his own balloon.

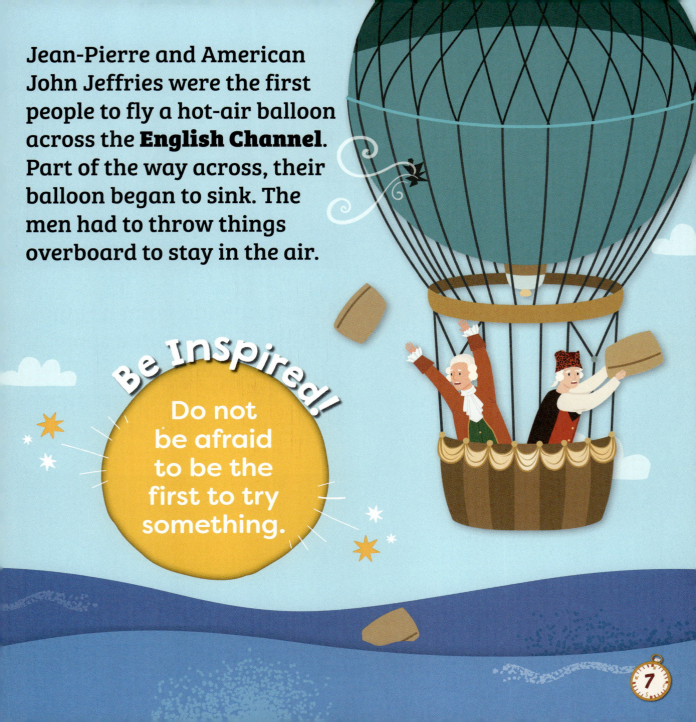

Jean-Pierre and American John Jeffries were the first people to fly a hot-air balloon across the **English Channel**. Part of the way across, their balloon began to sink. The men had to throw things overboard to stay in the air.

**Be Inspired!**

Do not be afraid to be the first to try something.

# HUGO ECKENER

**Born: 1868  Died: 1954**

A German man named Hugo Eckener **commanded** some of the first zeppelins. He flew these huge floating airships and trained other pilots.

The zeppelin was named after its inventor, Ferdinand von Zeppelin.

Hugo set a record traveling in an airship called the *Graf Zeppelin*. It took only 21 days for Hugo and his passengers to make it around the world.

**Be Inspired!**
Doing something with others can make it more special.

# ORVILLE WRIGHT AND WILBUR WRIGHT

Born: 1871   Died: 1948   Born: 1867   Died: 1912

American brothers Orville and Wilbur Wright made and flew the first **controlled** airplane.

The Wright brothers watched **gliders** to learn how to fly. Then, they built their plane. Their first flight lasted 12 seconds. After some practice, the brothers were able to fly for longer.

**Be Inspired!**
Keep practicing to get better at things you enjoy.

# BESSIE COLEMAN

**Born: 1892**
**Died: 1926**

Bessie Coleman was the first Black American and Native American woman pilot. She had to go to France to get her pilot's **license**.

Bessie learned a lot of risky airplane tricks. She could fly very close to the ground, flip upside down, and even make shapes in the air!

## Be Inspired!

Do what you love, even if no one has done it before.

# CHARLES LINDBERGH

**Born: 1902   Died: 1974**

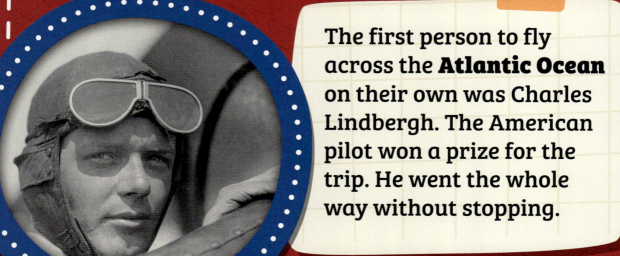

The first person to fly across the **Atlantic Ocean** on their own was Charles Lindbergh. The American pilot won a prize for the trip. He went the whole way without stopping.

Charles' flight took almost 34 hours.

To stay awake, Charles let cold air in through the windows. He arrived in France to find lots of people waiting for him, even though it was dark.

## Be Inspired!

Try to be independent and do things on your own!

# AMELIA EARHART

**Born: 1897  Died: Around 1937**

Five years after Charles flew across the Atlantic Ocean, another American pilot decided to try as well. Amelia Earhart became the first woman to make that airplane trip on her own.

Amelia faced many problems in flight. Still, she crossed the ocean faster than Charles did. Amelia's flight took less than 15 hours.

## Be Inspired!

Try not to panic when things go wrong.

# AMY JOHNSON

**Born: 1903**
**Died: 1941**

Amy Johnson was a British woman who flew about 11,000 miles (17,700 km) to Australia on her own. The maps she had to plan her trip weren't very good.

Amy planned her route by putting a ruler on simple maps.

# BERTRAND PICCARD AND BRIAN JONES

Born: 1958    Born: 1947

Bertrand Piccard is from Switzerland

Brian Jones is from England

Bertrand Piccard and Brian Jones were the first people to make a trip around the world in a hot-air balloon. It took them about 20 days.

# YOUR AIR ADVENTURE

Many people fly through the air every day. People have been on adventures in hot-air balloons, zeppelins, and airplanes. How would you choose to explore the world by air?

Draw your own flying machine. How many people can it carry? What kind of weather can it go through? Where would you like to go?

# GLOSSARY

**Atlantic Ocean** the ocean between Europe, Africa, North America, and South America

**commanded** was in charge of

**controlled** guided by a person

**desert** a place that gets very little rain and where few plants and animals can survive

**English Channel** the area of water between England and France

**gliders** aircraft without engines that can fly using only the wind

**license** a document that proves someone is allowed to do something

**sandstorm** a strong wind that carries lots of sand with it

**touring** traveling from place to place

# INDEX

airplanes 4, 10–11, 13, 16, 22
Atlantic Ocean 14, 16
control 10
desert 19, 21
France 12, 15
gliders 11
hot-air balloon 6–7, 20–22
license 12
plan 18
tricks 13
weather 19, 23
zeppelin 8–9, 22